"If you're like most church leaders I know, training and developing volunteers is one of your greatest challenges. When it comes to equipping small group leaders, Heather Zempel has done the homework for you. Heather not only knows what group leaders need to do but she knows how to do it. *Big Change, Small Groups* is a fantastic resource that you need to put in the hands of every small group leader in your church."

Jenni Catron,
Leadership Consultant, Author of *The 4 Dimensions of Extraordinary Leadership*

"Heather Zempel has produced a great resource! Small group leaders will be inspired, encouraged, supported, and challenged by *Big Change, Small Groups*. Written in an engaging style, this book offers profound insights into being an effective small group leader, and does it in a simple, easy-to-understand, and entertaining way. The book is small, but the ideas are big. I recommend it for anyone who is currently leading or thinking about leading a small group."

Steve Gladen,
Pastor of Small Groups, Saddleback Church, Author of *Small Groups With Purpose, Leading Small Groups With Purpose* and *Planning Small Groups With Purpose*

"Heather Zempel is no theorist. She's a legit practitioner who's led groups and led small group ministries and led them very well. Like Paul, she's left behind an ever growing wake of group members and group leaders she's loved, cared for, encouraged, and pointed toward Jesus; members "who can't tell their story without including her name." If you want your group leaders to learn to lead in this way, don't miss *Big Change, Small Groups*."

Mark Howell,
Groups Pastor, Blogger, Coach and Consultant

"This book is on point! Over the last 15 years, I have coached hundreds of small group leaders and used many valuable small group resources, and I can confidently say that this is now the first and best resource I will use to equip, strengthen, and encourage small group leaders. Heather's poignant insights, practical advice, and a well articulated proven process makes this book a must use resource for all small group leaders!

Steve Saccone,
Author of *Talking About God*

"Heather Zempel is a small groups guru with wisdom, insight, and best practices you can't afford to miss. Stop, drop, and read this immediately."

Margaret Feinberg,
Author of *Fight Back With Joy*

"Heather has done it again. Turning complex expectations into simple practices is a gift God has given her and she has most certainly used that gift on our behalf once more. This powerful, unpretentious, and profound guide for small group leaders will enhance each leaders ministry ten-fold. What you'll find between the front and back cover of this resource is all that is necessary for anyone to become an effective and transformational small group leader."

Rick Howerton,
Church Consultant serving 413 Churches in Kentucky,
Author of *A Different Kind of Tribe*

"I am so thankful my friend Heather Zempel once again engaged in the heavy lifting of writing a book on community. Heather lives it, leads it and as a result, gets it. *Big Change, Small Groups* will be a resource small group leaders come back to over and over again. It's that important. It's that helpful. It's that good."

Bill Willits,
Executive Director of Ministry Environments at North Point Ministries and Author of *Creating Community*

"As a new church plant, we are trying to find ways to grow our small groups and raise up leaders. Heather has created a practical how-to guide that is easy to start and hard not to finish. *Big Change, Small Groups* is practical, simple, and totally within our means to implement and share with leaders."

Bianca Juarez Olthoff,
Church Planter, Pastor, and Author of *Play With Fire*

Big Change, Small Groups
Published by Orange, a division of The reThink Group, Inc.
5870 Charlotte Lane, Suite 300
Cumming, GA 30040 U.S.A.

The Orange logo is a registered trademark of The reThink Group, Inc.

All Scripture quotations, unless otherwise noted, are taken from the *Holy Bible, New International Version®. NIV®.* Copyright © 1973, 1978, 1984 by International Bible Society. Used by permission of Zondervan.

Other Orange products are available online and direct from the publisher. Visit our website at www.WhatIsOrange.org for more resources like these.

ISBN: 978-1-63570-071-8

©2018 The reThink Group, Inc.

Writers: Heather Zempel
Lead Small Editing Team: Afton Phillips, Steph Whitacre
Art Direction: Ryan Boon
Project Manager: Nate Brandt
Design: FiveStone

Printed in the United States of America
First Edition 2017

2 3 4 5 6 7 8 9 10 11

08/10/18

**brought to you by the team that developed
LEAD SMALL**

DEDICATION

If you are reading this book, you are probably in the position of leading a small tribe of people. That's right, you are a small group leader. You have the courage to focus on a small community of people in order to take on a big challenge. You choose to invest—really invest—in a few lives.

This book is dedicated to you. You are the heroes of the church.

You are making a big difference
one discussion,
one lesson,
one snack,
one group meeting at a time.

Or maybe you're not a small group leader yet—you're still considering it. Someone has asked you to take that leap of being a small group leader.
Or you think it's something that might fit with your passion, skills, and schedule.

This book is also dedicated to you. We hope in these pages you will be ignited with a passion for making big change by investing in a few.

A FEW WORDS IN ADVANCE

So you're leading a small group of adults. Congratulations!

Maybe, like many others, you're wondering . . .
What exactly do you do?
Where do you fit in their lives?
What is your role?

And even more, *why*?

That might even be why you picked up this book.

If so, good news. This is your handbook, your user guide.

As you read, you will notice sections marked "Journal."
Benjamin Franklin said, "The shortest pencil is longer than the longest memory." The stuff we write down tends to stay with us longer. And the principles we process on paper seem to be absorbed more deeply. Most of what you read in this book may be forgotten two minutes after you close it. But the stuff you write down will stick.

Warning: If you are reading this on an e-reader, please don't mark on your screen with pen. You might have a little trouble getting it off. Instead, grab a spiral notebook, some sheets of paper, or even that old journal that someone gave you as a gift that you never used. Record your thoughts as you go along to make this book personalized to you.

So, read it.
Contemplate it.
Personalize it.

Let's get started.

table of contents

foreword

There's a good chance you're reading this because you either currently lead a small group of adults or you are considering it. Good for you! I wholeheartedly believe that adults—just like kids—need an awesome small group experience with a great leader. You may also be reading this because you don't feel 100 percent confident you're the right person for the job. Even better! Why? Because I'm convinced you're holding the right resource in your hands this very moment.

How, exactly, will this book help you fill the big shoes of a small group leader?

First, it shrinks an overwhelming role into four primary tasks. I believe as you dive into these four tasks, leading a group will suddenly seem much more doable. (In case you were thinking you must be all things to all people, forget it; nobody can or is.)

Second, Big Change, Small Groups explores our innate need for (and the power of) community: God created it; Jesus embodied it; the early church thrived because of it. An effective small group environment is an ideal place to develop authentic faith, impact others, and fulfill the last instructions Jesus gave us to go change the world. You play a significant part in making this happen for the adults you lead, for the glory of the God you serve!

Third, it encourages you to jot down your thoughts as you read. If you don't consider yourself a journaler, let me urge you to make the effort. In my experience, recording your thoughts leads to exploration, inspiration, and even motivation.

One reason I am convinced this is the right resource for you is because I know the person behind the words. Heather Zempel is a leader in every sense of the word who also happens to have a passion for helping others grow spiritually. Heather serves as our Pastor of Discipleship at National Community Church in Washington, DC, where she oversees small groups, directs leadership development training, and serves on our weekend teaching team. I'm not sure I know anyone more passionate about discipleship or more gifted at groups. The "community" in National Community Church wouldn't be what it is without her!

I am also convinced you can do this; you can "lead small." You know that what you do for a few has more potential than what you can do for many. You can be engaged and present in little ways that make a big difference. You can learn to see past the mess that may sometimes make its way into your group and wait patiently for the miracle. You can be the leader who makes a difference in the lives of the adults you lead. Yes, YOU!

And it may just change your life as well.

Mark Batterson
Lead Pastor, National Community Church
Washington, DC

big challenge.
small solution.

The last command Jesus gave His followers was

Go make disciples.
Of *all* nations.

Change the world.
Take the message everywhere.
Make sure people on the other side of the globe who speak different languages and live with different priorities know about Me.

Change the world in the same way I changed your life.

That was a seemingly impossible task for a small band of 120 Jews living under Roman occupation in the First Century. There were no cars, zero printing presses, and social media hadn't been invented.

Most of us would have started a campaign.
Launched a mass marketing strategy.
Organized a rally.

We would have done something big to meet Jesus' big challenge.
To gain a big following, you have to …
make a big, compelling, persuasive speech.
accomplish a big feat.
gather a large following of people.

Get noticed.
Get attention.
Get people talking.

Go big or go home.

But what if "go home" was actually the solution Jesus advocated?

It was a big challenge. But Jesus had a small solution.

The power of community. Leveraging the place where you live.

What we call leading small.

When God came to earth wrapped in the skin of His own creation, He did not call a press conference or organize a world tour or advertise five nights of revival at the Colosseum in Rome.

In fact, He never even went to the places of influence or power. Instead, He settled around the fishing villages on the Sea of Galilee and gathered twelve men around him. He did life with them and pointed out the character and mission of God along the way. He said, "Follow me. Do what I do the way I do it."

That was His strategy for changing the world.
It was a strategy followed by the apostle Paul. As Paul took the message of God to more and more distant cities, he started churches as small groups in homes.

Lydia's house.
Priscilla and Aquila's house.
Nympha's house.
Philemon and Apphia's house.

Paul told his young protégé Timothy, "And the things you have heard me say in the presence of many witnesses entrust to reliable people who will also be qualified to teach others." (2 Timothy 2:2).

In other words, here's how to get started. Just gather together some faithful people and share your life with them. And then encourage them to gather small groups around them.

Pass on the faith one small group at a time.
Change the world one small group at a time.
Fulfill Jesus' mission one small group at a time.

Within a few hundred years, these gatherings had so transformed their world that the entire empire was buzzing.

Two thousand years later, small bands of Jesus' followers still gather in homes, coffeehouses, work conference rooms, playgrounds, and church classrooms to experience the transformative power of community.

BIG CHANGE

HAPPENS

WHEN WE

LEAD SMALL.

leading small

"What *exactly* do you mean by leading small?"

That's a phrase we've picked up as we've seen the power of small groups with consistent leaders. We've seen it work for every age: from the preschoolers to kids to teens to grown-up groups like the ones we're talking about here.

What we do for a few will always have more potential than what we do for many.

That means we simply make a choice to invest strategically in the lives of a few over time so we can help them grow an authentic faith.

The idea of community is essential to the character of God. In fact, God exists as a community of Father, Son, and Holy Spirit. It's a theological construct called the Trinity that is impossible to grasp yet inextricably core to our understanding of the connection God wants us to pursue. The God we follow exists as a community in and of Himself.

To follow the heart of God, we must live in community. There are dozens of commands in Scripture that we cannot be obedient to outside the context of community.

They are the "one another" commands.

Love one another.
Serve one another.
Honor one another.
Forgive one another.

Accept one another.
Bear one another's burdens.

In John 13:35, Jesus said, "A new command I give you: Love one another. As I have loved you, so you must love one another. By this everyone will know that you are my disciples, if you love one another."

Jesus made it clear that our love for one another would send a clear and compelling message to the world.

Not our sermons
or books
or worship songs.

Instead,
The way we connect to one another.
The way we cultivate community.
The way we love.

In John 17, Jesus prayed that his followers would be "one." That just like He and the Father walked in inseparable community, those coming after Him would find strength, identity, and purpose within the context of community.

His reason? *"So that the world may believe that you have sent me (John 20:21)."*

Once again, community would be the catalyst for spreading his message and changing the world.

Small groups would be the engine for discipleship.
Small groups would be the fuel for spreading the message of Jesus around the world.
Small groups would be the crucible for building and growing authentic faith.

Jesus' last command cannot become our least concern.

It's not an overwhelming task if we choose to begin small.

We lead small to build big faith.
We lead small to generate lasting faith.
We lead small to produce authentic faith.

In every stage of life and stage of their faith journey, every person needs the kind of influence you have the potential to give.

But what exactly do you do?
What exactly is your role?

There is the potential to wear so many hats:

Pastor
Resident theologian
Counselor
Caregiver
Coach
Prayer warrior
Teacher
Best friend

And all with a touch of Martha Stewart hospitality.

How can one person be expected to be good at all of those things? You can't. But it's not your job to be all of those things to the people in your group.

That's why we've attempted to boil down the small group leader (SGL) mission to four primary tasks:

| **Be Present** | **Create a Safe Place** | **Make It Personal** | **Move Them Out** |

Even more, you will understand how these four strategies will encourage the personal, vibrant, passionate, tested, living, authentic faith needed to face our big challenge, and why the only way to fully invest in these strategies is by leading small.

So, let's change the world.

Oh, you still have a few questions? Okay, keep reading!

be present

CONNECT THEIR FAITH TO A COMMUNITY

In the beginning, God created.
At the sound of his voice, galaxies were hurled into orbit.
Light beamed from the heavens and waters covered the earth.
Valleys dug deep and mountains sprung high.
Birds flew in the air and fish swam in the seas.
Insects filled the ground and dinosaurs thundered across
the land.

And it was good.

Then God made man.
Adam.
The perfect image of God Himself. The masterpiece. The
magnum opus of all creation.
But . . .
It. Was. *Not.* Good.

Not yet at least.

Immersed in lush vegetation, living in paradise, surrounded by
every species of animal, Adam found himself alone.

Even though he was designed to be the perfect image-bearer
and reflection of the Creator . . .
Even though he was made to have direct community with God
himself . . .
Something was wrong.
He had no one like him—to talk to, to laugh with, to dance with.

What we might read as a hiccup in the creation story may be an intentional play by God to drive home an important idea:

WE WERE CREATED WITH

THE NEED FOR COMMUNITY.

So God made Eve.

And now, with man and woman together, God declared that His creation was *very* good.

Fast-forward thousands of years.
God came to Earth as man.
At the beginning of Jesus' ministry
He chose twelve guys.
He didn't invite the masses.

His goal was not to fill the largest amphitheater in Corinth.
He led thousands but chose to invest in, to do life with, a few.

Understanding the human need for community and its significance in our lives, Jesus surrounded Himself with a few deep relationships. In doing this, He connected the faith of the twelve. And after Jesus was no longer on Earth to lead them, the disciples were able to stay strong in their faith because it was connected to others.

Still not convinced? Let's go a step further.

Fifty years passed and Paul was busy setting up the Church in cities across the known world—building the Church around this concept of community.

The earliest churches had no buildings.
No pulpits.
No choirs or praise bands.

There were no kids' programs.
No student ministries.
No fall festivals or Easter outreaches.

There was simply community.

In Acts 2, we catch a glimpse of what the early church was doing. It says that they
met regularly
in the temple
(kind of like their regular church service)
and from house to house
(getting up close and personal).
They were devoted to
the apostle's teaching
(they were learning together)
to fellowship
(they were having fun, laughing, sharing,
doing life together)
breaking bread
(we church people have a long history
with the potluck)
and prayer
(connecting with God together).

Genuine, pure, tight-knit, nothing-to-hide, kill-my-best-goat-for-you kind of community.

The church wasn't a place. It wasn't a building or an event or an organization. It was a group of people whose lives had been changed by Jesus and who were on mission to spread His message and build His kingdom. Whenever the group gathered, the church thrived. Wherever the group gathered, the larger communities around them were impacted. Widows and children were fed. The poor were seen as equals. The sick were cared for. It was said that those in the Roman Empire would remark, "See how these Christians love one another."

When Paul wrote to the church in Thessalonica, he made a statement that reveals, almost defines, this early glimpse of community:

"So we cared for you. Because we loved you so much, we were delighted to share with you not only the gospel of God but our lives as well (1 Thessalonians 2:8)."

There it is.

Your job as an SGL.

You care.
You love.
You delight.

But most importantly, you share—not just the Gospel—but your life as well.

God *is* community—as Father, Son, and Holy Spirit.
God created us for community.
Jesus illustrated community.
The Church practiced community.

Therefore, connecting the faith of your few to a community is your primary goal. So, how do you create this community?

BE PRESENT.

When you choose to be present you

connect authentic faith.

When you choose to be present,

that means you . . .

Show up predictably.

Show up mentally.

Show up randomly.

1 Show Up Predictably

For most of you, showing up predictably means showing up weekly. For a few, it may mean bi-weekly or even monthly. But for most, it is showing up every week.
Being there.
Arriving on time.
Physically being present.

Showing up consistently and predictably establishes the foundation of a small group that foundation is trust.

You cannot lead a small group without trust.
You cannot build a community without trust.
And the first step to gaining the trust of your few is making sure they know you will show up consistently and predictably.

The recent college graduate needs someone they can call when they need some life wisdom.
The female executive needs someone to know that this season at work is high pressure and high stakes, but her relationships matter most.
The schoolteacher needs someone who will encourage them just a little bit more at the start of the school year.
The new dad needs someone who can show him how to clean a diaper explosion, wipe off the spit-up, and get a screaming kid to sleep all while tending to the needs of his thriving business.
The young stay-at-home mom needs someone who can string together actual sentences and relate to her many more-than-full-time jobs.

Everybody needs someone who knows their name and knows what's happening in their life.

Granted, you probably can't be all these things to all the people in your group. But you can lay that foundation. Establish that expectation. And create an environment in which people can be those things for each other.

Make your group a place where each person can play a role in making a difference in someone else's life.

Does it happen overnight? Does this kind of community happen the first time you meet? Is there a formula for creating it?

No.

But consistent, predictable presence steadily weaves the relational Velcro that will eventually create strong, healthy, and vibrant community.

To start building a framework of a group where everybody knows your name and cares about what's happening in your life, have them share:

Ask a different person to share their story each week as you launch a new group.
Ask each group member to share their week's high point and low point.
Ask people to share their hero, highlight, and hardship from childhood.

Or use an icebreaker question. Lean into icebreaker questions that are fun and reveal someone's history and personality. Try something like:

If you could go to any concert in the history of the world, what would it be?
What accomplishment, before the sixth grade, are you most proud of?
What three people have been most influential in your life?
What are your family's Christmas/Thanksgiving/Easter/Fourth of July traditions?
What was your favorite family vacation and why?

Journal ✎

It's time to grab a pen and record a few things about those in your circle. Go the extra step and bring your list to your next meeting to record important tidbits about your group members.

For bonus fun, write down a few icebreaker questions you can use in the upcoming weeks.

2 Show Up Mentally

Next, show up mentally. That means being fully present with those in front of you. Physically, mentally, emotionally, and spiritually.

Before you come to the group, make sure you're prepared.
If there is a lesson, make sure you've completed it.
If you need to have questions ready to ask, make sure they are thoughtful and have a progressive movement to them.
Move from questions surrounding

Facts (What did you read? What did you observe)
to
Opinion (What did you think about this? How did it make you feel? How do you reconcile these truths with what you experience in your own life?)
to
Action (What are we going to do about this? How can we make this practical?)

If a group is meeting at your home, make sure it is comfortable and inviting. If you are meeting in a public space like a coffeehouse or a restaurant, arrive early enough to grab a good spot. Regardless of where you meet, make sure it sends the message "we were expecting you."

Be prepared by praying.
Pray for your group members and the needs you know are present in their lives.
Pray that the time your group spends together would be beneficial and encouraging.
Pray that you, as the leader, would have wisdom, discernment, and grace as you lead.

While you are at the group, be present mentally by . . .
turning off your phone—or at least silence the rings and
notifications.

not thinking about work—it will still be there when you get back.

leaning in to listen—and not to make your next point.

Let your curiosity guide you. Be aware of what's being said,
what's being felt, and what's happening in the group.

Don't be so determined to get through a curriculum or a series
of questions that you miss a moment.

A moment for encouragement.

A moment to let some silence sit so new ideas can sink in.

A moment for someone else to speak up.

A moment to stop and pray.

Be engaged.

Journal

Here's the good news about showing up mentally: what you model, your group members will eventually begin to do too. At least, that's the goal. But it will be hard for them to be present with one another if they don't first experience you doing it.

Write down a few ways you can show up for the members of your group. Be specific.

Now, imagine the effect this can have on your group. Are there times when this has been a struggle for your group? What are some steps you can take to begin to eliminate this struggle?

3 Show Up Randomly

Once you start showing up predictably, your few will begin to expect it. Good. But what if, on occasion, you surprised them? What if you showed up at a time and place they weren't expecting?

When I was walking through a pretty confusing time of infertility, I only shared my experiences with a very small circle. A couple years later, I received a card in the mail from my friend Nina. It simply said, "I'm still praying." That was it. No lengthy prayers. No theological discourse. Not even a Bible verse. Just a simple reminder that I was not alone.

Many years and a toddler later, I still have that note. There is something about it that brings me courage and builds my faith when I go through any kind of challenging time because it is a reminder that

I
am
NOT
alone.

People are thinking about me outside of group. They are praying for me outside the scheduled prayer time. They are "with me" in my journey.

When we say "random" we don't mean haphazard. We mean showing up in very intentional but perhaps unexpected ways. Intersecting their life where it happens. Making small gestures that make a big impact.

Another time, I went to the hospital to visit a member of our church. When I arrived, it was standing room only. The room was packed with this member's small group, which had already figured out plans for meal delivery, care, and how they would be chauffeured home from the hospital.

That's the way the church should operate.

Help someone move.
Make a phone call to encourage someone before the big presentation.
Give a shout-out on social media.
Send a birthday card or an anniversary card.
Buy a small gift card for that person who always brings the snacks.
Shoot a text that says, "I'm still praying."
When invited, show up to their party or their kid's recital or concert or game or chess match.

It doesn't have to be big and earth-shattering. Again, it's about the power of small groups—being engaged and present in little ways.

Journal ✏️

Make a list of ways you can show up randomly in the lives of your group. Schedule times to implement your ideas.

....

....

....

....

....

....

....

....

....

....

....

....

....

....

These small connections may seem insignificant—and sometimes even inconvenient. But when you choose to be present in an unexpected way, outside of your weekly group time, you reinforce your group members' connection to the community you are creating. They have a greater sense of belonging because they feel cared for and connected.

And this sense of community will grow and encourage authentic faith when you . . .

Show up   **Show up**   **Show up**
predictably.   **mentally.**   **randomly.**

Your group will begin to trust. They will begin to open up. They will begin to do for others what you have done for them. They will begin to root themselves in the kind of community . . .

God designed them to need.
Jesus illustrated with the disciples.
the early church practiced regularly.

WHEN YOU CHOOSE TO BE PRESENT, YOU CONNECT AUTHENTIC FAITH.

create a safe place

create a safe place

CLARIFY THEIR FAITH AS THEY GROW

Small groups are messy places.

They are messy because they are about people hauling in their brokenness and baggage and dumping it into your living room. The mess can consist of sin mess, relational mess, and life mess.

It's the inevitable tension created when a group of different people with different personalities and different backgrounds come together in one place. The tension shows up in families. The tension shows up in groups of friends. And you can bet the tension will show up with your group.

The tension that shows up between
millennials and Boomers.
right brain feelers and left brain thinkers.
introverts and extroverts.
those who read Revelation literally and those who read it
metaphorically.

Some listen to country music and some listen to hip-hop.
Some get their news from Fox and some watch CNN.
Some will drink alcohol and some will abstain.
Some love Monday Night Football while others are glued to
Dancing With the Stars.
Some grew up in the church and some think a Judas Kiss is a
song by Metallica.

Of course, the tensions won't all be as surface as pop culture and sports. As you go deeper with your few, new, more difficult tensions will arise.

Life messes.

Marriage problems
Bad reports from the doctor
Downsizing at the factory
Children with emotional struggles
Aging parents

One of my guiding principles in small group ministry is found in Proverbs 14:14:

"Without oxen a stable stays clean, but you need a strong ox for a large harvest." (NLT)."

You can have a clean, calm, tension-free group if you are the only one in it.
But it won't be very productive.
To have a transformational group means opening the doors of the barn to let the wildlife in and letting the mess happen.

The small group at Corinth dealt with plenty of messes.

Separation and divorce
Egos
Incest
Fighting over doctrine
Idolatry
Lawsuits
People getting drunk while celebrating communion

Small groups are great. And then the people show up. It might not become apparent on that first night, but at some point, you will hit a wall of mess. And no amount of prayer, training, or Biblical study can prepare you for it.

Community is messy.
But mess may be the very thing that brings the transformation you want to see, the unity you want to nurture, and the tension that will stretch your group in healthy ways.

Messes can be incubators for miracles.

The moment you discover that community is messy will become the defining moment of your leadership.
We can run from it, ignore it, and pray that time and inertia will be our ally in making it go away.
Or we can lean in and wade into the mess and embrace the tension.

That's one of our most challenging tasks as an SGL.
To create a safe place to deal with mess and live in tension.

Your group will be watching
How you handle conflict.
How you handle difficult questions.
How you handle differences in personalities.
How you handle fears.
How you handle impossible situations.

You are the leader.
You can't sweep the mess under the rug or eliminate the tension.
But you can manage it.

You can demonstrate that the group is a safe place for mess.
You can communicate that the group is a place where it's okay to not be okay.

And the safer your environment is, the more your group will build their faith in the context of the circle.
A safe placing for struggling marriages.
For millennials who have questions
For exhausted parents
For the successful businessman who is facing his greatest career challenge

For the student who is doubting their faith
For the single mom who doesn't know how to balance the kids
and the job
For the adult who is deconstructing their faith
For the brand-new follower of Jesus who is excited about
everything and zealous to change the world but lacking in tact

In order to apply the challenging teachings of Jesus to the
impossible situations of our lives within the context of difficult
relationships, we have to be intentional to

CREATE A SAFE PLACE.

When you choose to create a safe place you help your few build authentic faith.

When you chose to create a safe place, that means you . . .

Lead the group.

Respect the process.

Guard the heart.

Lead the Group

You have your group and you are ready to enjoy the community of people who

think like you
talk like you
act like you

or

maybe you love the idea of diversity. You can't wait to be challenged by different opinions, entertained by varied personalities, and taught from unique perspectives. Until those differences go just a little too far.

Not to scare you too much too soon, but leading a group is challenging.

Here are four challenges that every leader faces.

The Expectation Challenge
Everyone joins a small group for a different reason.
Some participants are looking for a counseling group.
Some are looking for their best girlfriends.
Some are looking for other Bible scholars.
Some are desperately trying to find a way to connect to the church.
Some are just looking for some time away from the kids.

Some will make coming to group every single week the highest priority on their calendars while others may show up when it's convenient.

The expectations are all over the place.

As the SGL, you set the tone for expectation. Naming and managing the expectations from the beginning is critical.

The Conversation Challenge

Then there is the conversation challenge. Community is established through conversation, and it comprises the largest amount of time of your group experience. But there are so many different kinds of talkers.

There are fast talkers
Long talkers
No talkers
Rabbit chasers
Hijackers
Complainers and
Gossipers.

Establishing a framework for what's in-bounds and what's out from the beginning will help you navigate the minefield of talking challenges.

The Leadership Challenge

Next is the leadership challenge. It's easy to get overwhelmed.

Becoming a small group leader doesn't mean you've become the expert, but some people will assume you have all the answers, are always available to hear about their problems, and have perfected the Fruit of the Spirit in your life.

Take the pressure off.
It's okay to say, "I don't know," and, "What does everyone else think?"
It's okay to say, "Let's give that a week to think about."
It's okay to say, "No."

The Chemistry Challenge

Finally, there is the chemistry challenge. As we've already noted, your group will attract a wide range of interesting characters.

Thinkers and feelers
Internal processors and out-loud thinkers
Optimists and pessimists
Republicans and Democrats.

Creating community with such varied and fascinating types can be difficult, but it can also provide a richer environment for learning and growth when they learn to lean into one another.

These challenges are not problems to solve, but tensions to manage. And one way to manage them is to establish a framework of shared values right from the start.

Values of expectations
Values of prioritization and preparation
Values of engagement

Expectation challenges can be managed by talking about commitment levels. It might even mean drafting a document for people to read or sign so they understand
What they are committing to
For how long
With whom
How they are expected to prepare
And what contributions they are expected to make

Conversation challenges can be addressed by establishing rules of engagement and agreed-upon principles for how group members are going to communicate with one another.

In establishing rules of engagement,

Lead your group to value acceptance.
Lead your group to value confidentiality.
Lead your group to value honesty.

The way you handle relational tension sets the tone of acceptance. Safety can be destroyed by an eye-roll, a heavy sigh, or a forced smile.

You can consistently create a place of acceptance by

celebrating everyone equally.
shutting down gossip.
privately addressing individual issues as they arise.

And while it may not be realistic for everyone to fully accept each other at all times, the consistent attempt on your part will prove to your group they are in a safe place that values acceptance.

Safe places also build on confidentiality. What is said in group stays in group. It doesn't get listed as a prayer request in the church bulletin. It doesn't get talked about with other parents as you drop off your kids at school. It doesn't get mentioned on social media. Simply stating that confidentiality is a rule of engagement for your group won't stop breaches from happening, but emphasizing and even enforcing the promise of confidentiality will make every one of those breaches more serious. And that makes this safe place even safer.

FINALLY, VALUE HONESTY. CONTRIBUTE YOUR OPINION, YOUR THOUGHTS, YOUR FEELINGS, YOUR FRUSTRATIONS, AND YOUR ANGER.

Honesty is a way for your group to
Be themselves
Share doubts
Ask questions
Admit struggles

We could probably write a book just on that list alone and why each of those things is essential for building their faith, but let's just sum it up by saying:

- If they can't be their Monday-through-Saturday selves when they are in group, they will have a hard time applying their faith in everyday situations.
- If they can't share their doubts in community, they will dwell on them privately.
- If they can't ask the group their questions, they will take them to Google. And we all know how helpful that can be.
- If they don't admit their struggles to someone, they will never experience the power of bringing things to light in a way that facilitates freedom and forgiveness.

You, as the SGL, model honesty in the way you engage. You set the tone and the bar for the level of honesty the group will experience.

Have you ever personally struggled with the tension between honesty and inappropriate disclosure?

In order to create a safe place where your few feel they can be transparent, it's important to be honest about your own spiritual, personal, and relational struggles—to a point. Ask yourself:

How will this story benefit them?
What am I trying to accomplish?
Why am I sharing this?

The point to which you can push depends on the maturity, longevity, and connection of the group. You have a responsibility to be vulnerable in order to create a safe place. New followers of Jesus need to know the doubts you struggle with and the questions you have. But be wise in what you share, when you share, and how you share. Is it true? Is it encouraging? Can they bear it? Engage them at levels that are constructive and not destructive.

Journal

Take some time to think about these challenges to leading groups. Which will be most difficult for you to manage? What are some additional challenges you have experienced and would add to this list? How might these challenges serve to enhance community and transformation as opposed to being a hindrance to it?

Make a list of expectations you want to communicate up front. While it won't eliminate tension, it will help manage them as they come up as a result of differing expectations.

2 Respect the Process

One step forward, one step backwards, and two steps
sideways.
Repeat.

That's the path of spiritual growth. It's the recipe for community.
Discipleship is not linear.
Community is forged in the crucible mess.

Respect the process.

Respect for the convoluted, non-linear process of faith
development communicates that your group is a safe place.

There is no checklist for developing an authentic faith in your
group. In fact, there is
no finish line.
No plaque.
No medal.
No pronouncement, "Congratulations! Your group has now
achieved authentic faith!"

Instead, authentic faith is a continual process. It's not static. It
is the molding, crafting, shaping, and changing of faith through
time, life experience, and reflection.

The process of spiritual growth is more about the direction you
are moving in than a destination to arrive at.

Jesus said to *make* disciples—not find disciples. Making
disciples requires time, intentionality, and energy. It is hard
work. It is a process.

And this process isn't the same for everyone. Each individual is
different. There is no one-size-fits-all to making disciples.

As a small group leader, you should expect some difficult questions.

Some will ask,
"If God is so good, then why do bad things happen to good people?"

Some will complain,
"Why is Jesus so narrow-minded as to claim to be the only way to God? What about people who are good and devoted to their own religions? Is it possible more than one road leads to God?"

Others will wonder,
"If Sunday is a day of rest, where does football fit in?"

Still others will need to understand,
"If God made man the day after He made animals, what about dinosaurs?"

We have to validate those questions. Otherwise, we will communicate that church is not a safe place to bring them but rather a place you come when you are already confident about your faith.

Sometimes the Bible is confusing. Sometimes God doesn't behave the way we want him to. Sometimes people raise questions that ruffle our theological feathers.

Instead of giving into that restless determination to make sure that everyone knows the *right* answer, consider validating the question.

"That's a great question."
"What does everyone else think about that?"
"Has anyone else ever wrestled with that?"
"Anyone have a thought about that?"

I believe the Bible is the foundation and filter for our life and beliefs, and therefore should be the foundation and filter for our groups.

"All Scripture is God-breathed and is useful for teaching, rebuking, correcting and training in righteousness, so that the servant of God may be thoroughly equipped for every good work." (2 Timothy 3:16-17)

The Bible is trustworthy, inspired, and authoritative in matters of life and faith. Part of your job is to connect the faith of our group to the timeless truth of Scripture. Be sure to open your Bibles together and talk about what it says. Wrestle through it. Pray through it. Even argue through it.

Help people wrestle through questions of faith for themselves. Model for them how you connect the Scriptures to your life. Your goal isn't to give correct answers to all of their questions, as though you were some brilliant walking, talking biblical encyclopedia.

Don't miss this:
You don't have to have all the right answers in order to be an SGL.

You just have to be willing to be a tour guide and go on a journey of discovery with people.

There is a big difference between being a travel agent and acting as a tour guide. Travel agents sit in the climate-controlled comfort of an office, sit behind a desk, and give you brochures telling you where to go, how to get there, what to do once you're there, and what you might see along the way. They may or may not have even been there before but they can tell you all about it and give you accurate answers to your questions.

Tour guides are different. They lace up the hiking books, strap on the pack, and go on the journey with you. Tour guides have trekked the trail before and can interpret the path for you along the way. They don't just warn you of possible dangers; they help you walk through them. While travel agents know a lot of information, tour guides have information that has been discovered in the process of experience.

What does this mean practically? We can't just talk about prayer in our small groups; we've got to do it with people. We can't just complete a workbook on serving our community; we've got to get out there and do it. We can't just explain to someone the best way to lead a group; we've got to do it alongside them. And we can't just give quick answers to complicated questions. We have to allow the process to take people on a spiritual journey of discovery and transformation.

And speaking of questions, the questions that you ask have great potential to bring transformation. Questions are more memorable, more stretching, and more transforming than teaching. I've discovered you can go to deeper places when you ask questions. The right question at the right time can make someone unzip their heart and crave encouragement and correction. I always keep a handful in my back pocket:

- Where do you see God most at work in your life?
- What is the biggest challenge you are facing right now?
- What fruit of the Spirit is most abundant in your life? The least?
- If you knew you could not fail, what would you attempt?

Good SGLs are skilled at the craft of constructing powerful questions and have cultivated the art of listening.

Respect the process of transformation, and they will learn that just because they have questions or doubts, it doesn't mean they have lost their faith. It just means, like you, they are in the middle of the unique process of clarifying and building authentic faith.

Journal

Faith is a process not just for your few, but you, too. What are your struggles with faith? What questions would you ask God if he were right in front of you? How can you have genuine conversations about these kind of faith questions with your small group?

....

....

....

....

....

....

....

....

....

....

....

....

....

3 Guard the Heart

Faith is personal.
We often process the most difficult times in our lives through
the filter of faith. Which is why, as an SGL, you should expect
some pretty tough, even shocking things to be revealed during
small group time—things that will create emotional tension.

When I was in my mid-twenties, I led a group for young
professionals. It was full of high caliber, high capacity leaders.
They were fun. They were hungry. They were committed.

We didn't get very far into our study of spiritual disciplines
before we discovered that

an apprentice leader was sleeping with his girlfriend.
an entrepreneur was engaged in shady (at best) and illegal (at
worst) business practices.
a girl spiraled into a chasm of depression as she tried to
process the physical and emotional abuse that had been
heaped on her as a child.

We waded through the pain of sins they had committed and
sins committed against them.

I thought I was a terrible SGL. I felt hopeless and helpless. Had
I not prayed enough? Had I not been engaged enough in their
lives? What was I supposed to do?

The Holy Spirit dropped the idea that perhaps they simply
had found a safe place for these sin messes, life messes, and
relational messes to be revealed and healed.

My role wasn't to clean it up.
That would be the role of the Holy Spirit. My role was to
continue to create that safe place where they were accepted,
valued, loved.

My role was to guard the heart.
Since that time, I have navigated many difficult situations with those in my groups.

Divorce
Job transitions
Lost pregnancies
Sexual harassment in the workplace
Near-death accidents
Deaths of parents and children
A small group leader later walking away from the faith

The list is long.

In walking through situations like these, I often try to ask myself the following questions:

Is this a …

sin mess (someone missing the mark of God's ways)

a relational mess (inevitable tension that happens when people of different temperaments, opinions, and cultures try to live in community)

or a life mess (heartaches and heartbreaks caused because we live in a broken world)?

Is this a problem to solve or a tension to manage?

What questions do I need to ask to ensure I have a complete picture?
Does this need to be addressed inside the group or one-on-one?
How do we all find an opportunity to grow in this and through this?

Above all else, how do we ensure they feel loved, valued, respected, and wanted?

There are times when guarding the heart will mean we need to get some help from the outside.

Your job is to live in the tension between respecting confidentiality and knowing when you are walking above your pay grade. For this reason, we always put a disclaimer on confidentiality. There is no way for an SGL to promise complete confidentiality. Part of creating a safe place means protecting your group. In some cases, the best way to protect your group is for the leader to walk a group member through a process that transcends the simple bounds of confidentiality. There are times when someone needs pastoral care, a counselor, or a recovery group. When such escalation is necessary, the leader shouldn't go it alone. Start with the group member, ask permission to involve someone with more experience or wisdom, then make this part of your journey together. Proceed in such a way that the group member feels protected, nurtured, guided, honored, companioned and not abandoned.

I encourage leaders to look out for hurts, habits and hang-ups. And when you find them, help those people to seek out opportunities and environments for recovery.

I also encourage them to be aware of trials, trauma, and tragedy that may need special support structures.

While your group cannot revolve around one person's addiction or trauma, you can be an encouraging and supporting community that helps them get the support and recovery they need and walk alongside them during the very difficult process.

Journal ✏

Make a list of some of the current messes you are navigating in your group. Identify if they are primarily sin messes, relational messes, or life messes. List some ideas of how you personally can be present, respect the process, and guard the heart during this season). How might the group be able to rally around the individual?

Are there any messes that you don't have the experience or insight to manage? If so, write down a few actions steps to getting outside help. If not, what might be some examples of messes that require outside help.

Remember, in order to Create a Safe Place you have to

Lead the group.   **Respect the process.**   **Guard the heart.**

Then your group will have the opportunity to open up in the small group environment and build their faith in a way they never could if you were leading big.

WHEN YOU
CHOOSE TO
CREATE A SAFE PLACE,
YOU CLARIFY
AUTHENTIC
FAITH.

make it persona

make it personal

INSPIRE THEIR FAITH BY YOUR EXAMPLE

"Follow my example, as I follow Christ." That's the kind of statement that gets the apostle Paul labeled with words like "arrogant" and "egotistical." But that's the instruction he gave to the church at Corinth.

Follow me.
Imitate me.
Do what I do.
I'll follow Christ and you copy me.

Why didn't Paul just take himself out of the equation and tell people to follow Jesus? Why did he establish himself as the object of focus for his disciples instead of Jesus himself?

Perhaps he recognized that people needed an example, a role model, a flesh-and-blood picture of Jesus that made His character, ways, and mission of visible and tangible.

When we step into a leadership role, we are basically saying the same thing Paul said, "Follow me as I follow Jesus."

Because we aren't the resident theologian.
We aren't the pastor.
We aren't the licensed counselor (at least not most of us).
We aren't the Bible scholar.

We are the small group leader.

We are saying:

Do life with me as I live it.
Grow your faith with me as I grow mine.
Learn as I learn.
Follow me as I follow Jesus.

On one hand, that relieves tremendous pressure. It means . . .

We don't have to know exactly what to do when the guy in our group goes bankrupt.
We aren't expected to know exactly how to counsel when one of our group member's kids announces they want to live as a different gender.
We don't have to take responsibility for helping the alcoholic break free from addiction.

Being a small group leader isn't primarily about the information we give,
but the invitation we offer.
An invitation into a life together.
Stumbling together,
learning together,
failing together,
celebrating together,
growing together.

Follow me as I follow Jesus.

While it is definitely a release of pressure to know that we don't have to have all the answers, we are still saying, "Follow my example." And that's hard. Sometimes it's actually easier to give good answers than to be a good example.

It's not about information. It's about invitation.

In Romans, Paul exhorts those who have a leadership gift to steward it well. We cannot just hope to become a good leader or even pray to become a good leader... we must work hard to become the kind of leader that is worth imitating.

As an SGL, you have to be a leader worth following. And that begins by leading yourself well.

Your group has a front-row seat to your life. The question is, what are they watching? Is it just a show? Or is it a real-life adventure pursuing God? What if watching your personal growth could be their front-row seat to what God wants to do in their lives?

The way you live your life communicates more than the way you lead your group.

This chapter isn't about what you do during group time. It's about what you do in the other 166 hours in your week.

If you want your group to have healthy relationships, they need to see it in you.
If you want your group to set boundaries, they need to see it in you.
If you want your group to be confident in who God made them to be, they need to see it in you.
If you want to see your group pursue their relationship with Jesus through prayer and Bible reading, they need to see it in you.

MAKE IT PERSONAL.

When you choose to make it personal you inspire authentic faith.

When you choose to make it personal that means you . . .

Live in Community.

Set Priorities.

Be Real.

Live in Community

The first step in leading yourself well is to live in community.
That sounds like a line from the how-to manual of the
Department of Redundancy Department. After all,

You are leading a small group
Creating community
Inviting others to deeper relationships.

But, the problem is that we can get so busy creating community
for other people that we fail to experience it ourselves.
We need to regularly evaluate how we are relating to the
community we have formed.

Am I fully engaged?
Am I fully transparent?
Am I fully present?

Is this a group where I feel known by others?

As a leader, it's also important that you build community
outside the context of the group itself. Make sure there is

Someone investing in you,
someone investing beside you,
and someone you are investing in.

We see examples of these relationships throughout the Bible.

Every Timothy had a Paul.
Every Elisha had an Elijah.
Every John Mark had a Peter.

Who is investing in you?
Leaders have other leaders investing in them.

Who is your Paul? Who are those who are investing in you

either directly or indirectly? Direct investors are those who know you, pray for you, encourage you, and challenge you. It might be a pastor, another small group leader who is a step ahead of you, or a mentor.

You can also find indirect investment. Leaders are learners and seek wisdom from across time and distance, like from books, podcasts, or blogs.

Who is investing beside you?
In addition to people who are investing in you, there are also people investing beside you.

Every David had his Jonathan.
Every Paul had a Barnabas and Silas.
Every Esther had a Mordecai.

Those who lead alongside us …
to encourage us.
to troubleshoot with us.
to share war stories with us.

They bring value to our lives because they are in the trenches with us. We find solidarity, understanding, and camaraderie with them. We can help one another grow.

Who has permission to ask anything at any time about any area of your life?
Who knows you best but loves you anyway?
Who brings a higher perspective when all you can see are the problems right in front of you?

Who are you investing in?
In other words, who is following you?

If you think you are leading and no one is following you, then perhaps you are just taking a walk. While you can't invest deeply in every person in your group, you should invest deeply in one or two. To raise up another person who can lead like you lead, create community like you create community, and make disciples like you make disciples.

Is there a person or two that you are intentionally developing to do the work you are doing?
To launch a group.
To lead a group.
To create more communities for people to connect.

To develop new leaders, look for people who are faithful, available, and teachable.

Do they show up?
Do they indicate a desire for leadership?
Do they demonstrate a desire to keep growing, keep learning, and keep stretching themselves?
Are they hungry and humble? Do they have hustle?

Great leaders have someone investing in them, other great leaders investing beside them, and emerging leaders coming behind them.

You need a Paul—someone investing in you.
You need a Barnabas—someone doing life and leadership with you.
You need a Timothy—someone you are raising up to lead like you.

Leaders live in community.

Journal ✏️

Write out the names of the people who challenge and encourage you.

 Set Priorities

Leaders make it personal by setting priorities. While leading a small group is certainly a bigger commitment than two hours every Tuesday, it's impossible to be available to everyone 24/7.

For most of us, there will always be more demand on our time than there are hours in the day.
There will always be more needs to address than we have the relational or physical capacity to meet.

One of the best things you can do for your group—and for yourself—is to make your priorities clear. They need to see what you value. And when they see the way you prioritize your life, it might even inspire your few to think about their own priorities.

Making it personal means setting spiritual priorities and relational priorities.

Spiritual priorities come in the form of habits.
Daily disciplines.
Personal practices.

Over time these habits help you know Jesus more and look a little more like Him.
We think that these five faith practices are a good place to start:

Read the Bible.
Talk to God.
Share Your Faith.
Be Generous.
Rest.

Read the Bible

Reading the Bible begins with picking a time, making a plan, and marking it up.

Picking a time means setting aside a particular time and place for reading your Bible.

Making a plan means being intentional and strategic about what you are reading and how much you are reading. If you open up your Bible, start reading in Genesis and continue to read along linearly, you are likely to tank out in Leviticus. We also shouldn't just play Bible roulette, opening up to random text and reading it because we will miss context and continuity of its message.

Be intentional.
Be strategic.
Make a plan.

If you need help, check out the Bible app and choose one of their made-for-you plans.

Finally, mark it up. Underline words and phrases that jump out to you. Highlight whenever you see a name of God or attribute of His character. Make comments. Ask questions. Don't just read it.
Engage it.
Wrestle it.
Question it.

Talk to God

Prayer is about making a plan, being real, and writing it down.

Making a plan means being intentional and strategic about when and how you are praying. Maybe you need to establish one daily prayer time. Maybe you want to utilize meal times. Maybe you want to put alarms on your phone to prompt you to pray at certain times of the day. Find a rhythm that works for you.

Be authentic. Don't use big theological words. Don't go King James English. Just talk. The way you normally talk. Ask questions. Express emotions. Tell Him what you love about Him. Petition Him for what you need. Express excitement and gratitude for your blessings. Be you.

Write it down. A lot of times, we can't thank God for answered prayers because we don't even remember we prayed them. Write down the people and situations you are praying for.

Share Your Faith
Know what you believe and why you believe it.

This doesn't mean you need to have every answer to every argument. It simply means having a faith that is real to you and you are willing to share with others.

It means inviting others into your faith story.
Inviting friends to church.
Sharing stories of how God has intersected your life in real ways.

Be Generous
Live with an open hand and an open calendar.
Share your resources with those who might need them more.
Give to the poor.
Buy lunch for someone experiencing homelessness.
Help an elderly neighbor run errands or clean their home.
Go serve on a missions team.
Be generous with the hours in your day, the passion in your heart, the skills in your hands, and the money in your pocket.

Rest
One of the most overlooked and under-practiced spiritual disciplines is rest.

God created for six days and rested on the seventh.
God commanded His people to work for six days and rest on the seventh.

We see a rhythm of work, rest, and play throughout the Scriptures. Find a way to make rest a priority in your life. Pick a time, make a plan, and guard it.

Ask yourself the following questions:
What recharges me?
What fills my tank?
What are things that I want to do—not that I need to do?
What makes me enjoy God more?

Those questions help you identify your unique approach to rest.

Then, you have to guard it. Everyone else has a wonderful plan for your life. If you don't control your calendar, then your calendar will control you.

The only way you can effectively discuss authentic faith with your group members is if you are experiencing authentic faith in your own life.

You can't encourage others to read their Bibles if yours is currently being used as a coaster on your coffee table or collecting dust by your bed.

You can't emphasize the power of prayer if the only time you pray is before dinner or when you cry for help before a big meeting.
You can't challenge your group to invite others to church if they don't see some new people by your side.

You can't push your group to live out faith in their lives if you aren't being generous with your own.

So set spiritual priorities.

In addition to spiritual priorities, set **relational priorities**. You cannot be equally accessible to everyone at every time.

You can please all of the people some of the time. You can please some of the people all of the time. But you can't please everyone all of the time. (To give credit where credit is due, various iterations of that quote have been credited to Abraham Lincoln, Mark Twain, P.T. Barnum, and an English monk-poet from 500 years earlier. Whoever originally said it, we know they weren't too worried about making everybody happy all the time.)

The point is to be intentional and thoughtful in whom your priorities should be.

You will cheat someone.

Someone in your life is going to get cheated.
Someone in your life is not going to get all of the time with you that they want.
Someone in your life is not going to get your full attention.
Someone is not going to get the best of you.

Who is that going to be?

On the surface it sounds terrible and maybe even unbiblical.
But prioritizing the right people in the right way might be the most Christ-like thing you do as a leader. Because Jesus prioritized. He was not equally available or accessible to everyone.

We tend to cheat the people who are closest to us because we think they are the ones we can make it up to the most quickly and easily.

They are the ones who have to love us.
They are the ones who aren't going anywhere.
And so we cheat them because it's easy.
We cheat our spouse, our kids. We tend to abdicate the roles that no one else can do.

Several years ago I had dinner planned with three friends. We had all met in a small group a few years earlier and now we were all leading our own. We tried to meet up once a month to learn from one another, grow together, and encourage one another.

Right before the dinner, I got a call from someone in the group I had currently been leading. There was a problem they needed help managing and a conversation they needed to have.

It was important, but not urgent.
It was critical, but not an emergency.

Because I am a bit of a people pleaser (and sometimes confuse small group leadership with my own little messiah complex), I found myself about to say, "I will meet you right away." Before those words escaped my mouth, the Holy Spirit gently nudged me, "Heather, you can't meet every need at every moment. If you don't prioritize time with those who are investing in you, you will eventually have nothing to give to the people who are looking to you."

Granted, there are many times I've moved personal plans or shifted personal priorities to be available to my group. But sometimes, we have to realize that saying "no" to a good thing allows us to say "yes" to a better thing.

There are people in your life that should always come before your group. Yes, you heard that right: your group should be *a* priority, but not *the* priority.

True, you should probably put them before your Facebook fan group, mailman or Starbucks barista, but sometimes having a date night with your spouse, choosing to take your kids to the park, picking up a friend with a flat tire, skipping group to celebrate your mom's 60th birthday, or leaving a small group retreat because your sister is in labor says more than always putting your group first.

You need to focus on the important relationships in your life because no one can be the spouse, parent, friend, child, or sibling that you are. And when you put significance on those people in your life, you are modeling healthy relationships for those in your group.

You are a physical, living, breathing example of someone who dates their spouse,
spends quality time with their children,
is there for their friends,
respects and honors their parents,
and values their siblings.

Make a decision ahead of time about who you are going to prioritize.

And when you DO have to cheat those most important to you, acknowledge it, talk about it, and minimize it.

You can't encourage your group to nurture healthy community or pursue good relationships if you aren't modeling that in your own life.

So set relational priorities.

Journal ✐

It's impossible to live by your spiritual and relational priorities if you never decide what they are.

Take a moment to make some plans for Bible reading, prayer, and rest.

What are some ways you can be practically generous with the resources and time that God has given to you?

Be Real

If you try to be someone in your circle that isn't consistent with who you really are when you aren't in your circle, you will eventually be found out by the ones you lead.

Be real about your struggles.
Be real about your faith.
Be real about your fears.
Be real about your joys.

Authenticity is one part humility and one part integrity.

Humility is an accurate estimation of oneself.
It does not mean thinking less of yourself, it means thinking of yourself less.
It's being willing to be known for who you really are.
Humility acknowledges weaknesses and strengths.

I played softball in my younger days and since we are talking about humility, I say this in all humility: I was good. I accumulated the most votes for the t-ball All Star team. I was a cracker jack shortstop and nothing got by me on third base. When I entered middle school, I finally got to show off my skills to the high school girls. My dad had been coaching me since I was in t-ball and I just knew he was as excited to show me off to the big girls as I was to show off for them. On the first day of practice, he sent me to left field. LEFT FIELD.

Outfield was not where you wanted to be placed, even if you were playing PeeWee ball. That's where the sub-par athletes played. And when I say "athlete," I use that term very generously. I'm talking about the kids that didn't care a lick about being on the team, the kids who were there because their parents made them, the kids that got distracted by the planes flying overhead, or the worm that just popped its head out of the ground. Those kids were safe in the outfield because no one ever hit out there. Infield was where the action was.

Particularly the left side of the infield. I loved the speed, the thrill of the double play, the fast reflexes as the ball zipped down the baseline and the quick throw to first base. I couldn't wait to show off my skill in the high school league.

Left field? I thought, clearly, my dad must hate me. Or he no longer believed in me. Obviously he was trying to teach me a lesson. There could be no other explanation. Seeing the disdain on my face, he gave me a stern, but reassuring, look that said, "You will thank me one day. And that day will be soon."

But Dad knew something I didn't know. In high school, girls can hit.
Hard.
And they usually pulled it to the left side of the field.

In one magical year, the entire game changed, and the new position of choice was left field. What dad knew that I didn't was that I would love left field more than third base because left field was the place where all the action would happen. I couldn't see into the future, but Dad could.

And Dad knew where I would come most alive—where my gifts would be best used.

Humility embraces the place the Father assigns.

Even when we don't like it or don't understand in the moment.

We have to understand that God created us uniquely and knows best. And we can be most ourselves when we humbly accept what He has given to us.

The gifts.
The opportunities.
The strengths.
The talents.

Be real about who you are.
Be real about who you are not.
Be real with your questions and doubts and uncertainties.
Be real with your strengths and your weaknesses.
Be real with your struggles and your success.

Be real by walking in humility.

Let's talk about that other part: integrity.

Are you the same person online as you are offline? Are you the same person on the platform as you are off the platform? Are the different parts of your life integrated? Do they make sense together? That's where you find authenticity.

In 2005, entrepreneur Colin Dowse began to make and market spray on mud for city-dwellers who drove 4 x 4s and wanted to give the impression that they had spent the weekend out in the country. He said, "With spray-on mud, they can make it look like they've been off-road instead of just driving to the shops and back." According to the company's website, spray-on mud can help give your friends, family and neighbors the impression you've just come back from a day's shooting, fishing, or visiting friends who live on a farm."

We all recognize how ridiculous that is, right?

Yet how many of us show up on Sunday with our spray-on worship faces?
With spray-on holiness?
With spray-on generosity?
With spray-on enthusiasm?

(By the way, do you know that the word enthusiasm is derived from two Greek words which mean "in God." En and Theos, In God. Pretty cool huh?)

Integrity means that our Sunday morning lives are integrated with our Monday morning and Friday night lives.

What masks are you wearing?
What brand are you trying to protect?
What image are you trying to polish?

Our brand, our Image, and our profile pic will be reduced to spray-on mud unless our lives are first integrated with the life of Christ—when the different components of our lives are integrated with one another.

Here are some questions to consider when thinking through our character:

How well do I treat people from whom I can gain nothing?
Am I the same person in the spotlight, around friends, and alone?
Do I quickly and freely admit when I've made mistakes and take responsibility for them?
Do I have an uncompromising moral compass for decisions or do I allow circumstances to determine my choices?
When I have something to say about people, do I talk to them or about them?

Be real.
Be a leader worth following
while holding on to who you really are.

Journal

Write down the names of a few people you are currently investing in and inviting or hoping to invite to church.

Some relationships are more important than others. Have you ever really thought about that? On a piece of paper, list the relationships in your life that you should put first—even before your few.

Choosing small group community helps you keep your world manageable. It allows you to focus on staying real in your own faith. When you focus on the circle closest to you, you have time and margin to

Live in Community   **Set Priorities**   **Be Real**

WHEN YOU
MAKE IT PERSONAL,
YOU INSPIRE
AUTHENTIC
FAITH.

move them out

ENGAGE THEIR FAITH IN A BIGGER STORY

The final command Jesus gave His followers began with the word "go."
The message of the Gospel compels us to take action.
To move.
To change.

That's also the mission of our group.

No matter how tight your community has become.
No matter how much you love one another.
No matter how much you have grown during your time together.
No matter how much you can't imagine anything changing.

Don't get comfortable.
Don't get complacent.
Don't settle.

There is more.

Get ready to move.

The book of Deuteronomy is a re-telling of the Exodus story of the Israelites. In verse 6 of the first chapter, God gives instructions to his people at Mount Horeb: "You have stayed long enough at this mountain. Break camp and advance into the hill country of the Amorites."

That mountain was familiar. It was known.
It was their place. Their security. Their home.

Also known as Mount Sinai, it was the place where God had delivered the Ten Commandments to His people.

It was a special place. A memorable place. A historical place.

But it was time to move.
It wasn't easy to move. It took courage. It took willpower. And it probably took a little blood, sweat, and tears.

The Bible is full of these kinds of stories.

Nehemiah had to leave his court-appointed position and travel back to Jerusalem in order to rebuild the walls.
Joseph and Mary had to make a journey to Bethlehem.
Jesus had to go through Samaria to encounter the woman at the well.
Peter had to step into the Gentile centurion's home to share the Gospel.
Paul had to leave Antioch to plant churches around the Roman Empire.

We were created by someone larger than ourselves for a story bigger than our own.
And that means those we lead were created for a story that is larger than our group.

As a leader, we should be constantly asking, "What is the next step?"

We want people to grow, to change, to move, to begin the next chapter of the story that God is writing in their lives.

While it probably sounds counterintuitive, one of the primary roles of the leader is to **move them out.**

When you choose to move them out you engage

authentic faith.

When you choose to move them out,

that means you . . .

Move them to someone else.

Move them to be the church.

Move them to what's next.

① Move Them to Someone Else

In the introduction of this book, we looked at an encouragement that Paul gave to his young protégé, Timothy:

"And the things you have heard me say in the presence of many witnesses entrust to reliable people who will also be qualified to teach others." (2 Timothy 2:2)

It was an example of the scale of magnitude of impact that we are invited to play in the story of God.

But it's also an example of the invitation.
An invitation to those in our group
to also become leaders worth following.

When Jesus told His followers to go change the world, the only strategy He gave was for people to impact neighborhoods.

You are reading this book.
You are leading.
You are making disciples
because Paul and Timothy and others dared to believe that
Jesus' seemingly crazy strategy could work.
And it did.

Paul to Timothy to faithful men to others and on and on through generation after generation to us.

The only way to truly measure discipleship is by multiplication.
By reproducing.
By raising up other people who do what you do.
To create other small communities where people can be known, can connect, can grow.

Always be on the lookout for someone else who can lead small groups, like you. Look for people who are F.A.S.T... no, not like Speedy Gonzales or the Road Runner... but like this:

F **Faithful.** Look for people who are committed to the group and committed to Jesus. They show up. They don't look for the credit. They don't have to be the center of attention. They do little things like they are the big things and don't make a big deal about it.

A **Available.** Look for people who are consistently on time, willing to take ownership, and ready to serve. Some people have the potential to be great small group leaders, but they just aren't in a season of life where they have the margin in their calendar or the relational Velcro to do it. So look for people who are available and willing to be available to others.

S **Servant-hearted.** Leadership isn't about being the smartest person in the room, the spiritual giant whose prayer life dwarfs all others, or the person who makes all the decisions. Leaders follow the way of Jesus to serve others. Look for someone who cares about others and is willing to make someone else's good their highest priority.

T **Teachable.** Look for people who have humble hearts and hungry minds. Being a small group leader doesn't mean you have all the answers. The best small group leaders are the ones who relentlessly pursue the right questions. They aren't know-it-alls but people who want to learn and grow. They are more learners than teachers.

When you find that someone who is F.A.S.T., start the process of moving them on to someone else. Move them on to leading their own group.

Here are a few steps in that process:

Drop some hints.
Let them know you see potential in them. Be specific in your encouragement. Maybe they are great at bringing people into the conversation. Maybe they ask great questions. Maybe they make others feel welcome. Maybe they are great at encouraging. Point that out.

Work through this book with them.
Clarify the role of the leader, explain to them how you make it safe, demonstrate to them how you make it personal, and cast a vision for moving them out.

Give them more ownership in the group.
Let them lead an icebreaker or part of the discussion or the prayer time. Give them feedback.

Help them find a group to lead.
At some point, it's time to completely move them out. If your group is connected to a local church, there may be a process in place for that to happen. Otherwise, it might mean a few from your existing group moves out with the new leader to help begin a new group. It may mean finding a completely different few. It might be a few in your church, in their workplace, in their neighborhood, at their local coffeehouse, or at their gym.

Celebrate.
Throw a party. Commission them with prayer. Speak words of encouragement over them.

Your job is to lead a few.
It's also your job to lead a few to lead a few.
Cast a vision for disciples who make disciples who make disciples.
Encourage your few to find a few of their own.

Move them on to someone else.

Journal ✐

Make a list of 2–3 people in your few who might make good leaders themselves.

_____

_____

_____

_____

_____

_____

_____

_____

_____

_____

_____

_____

_____

_____

_____

Outline 1–2 ways you would like to see each of them
develop as F.A.S.T. leaders.

Make a plan for talking to them about transitioning into leadership.

② Move Them to Be the Church.

A church isn't a building or an event or an organization.
It's a group of people bonded together by a relationship
with Jesus,
who are committed to doing life together.
You can't go to church because you are the church.

The same can be said of your group.
Group isn't just a time slot on your calendar.
It's not just an event you attend.
It's not just a place you go once a week.

It's a group of people doing life together and growing together.

Move your few from going to group to being a group.

Here's the thing: they won't move from going to group to being
a group until you give them ownership. Give them significance.
Give them a role.
Give them a responsibility.
Make it impossible for them to miss without being missed.

It's about moving people from being consumers to contributors.
Responsibility and relationship keep people engaged.

Find the person who bakes the best cookies (or the person who
is best at recruiting those people) and commission them to be
the hospitality leader.

Identify the person who takes the best notes when people are
sharing prayers requests and make them the prayer leader. Ask
them to email their list out once a week.

Pay attention to the person who loves to have fun and include
as many people as possible and ask them to be the community
builder for your group, to plan activities outside of group time
for fun.

Listen to the people who ask really good questions. Make them discussion co-leaders.

Listen for the people who ask really creative and fun questions. Put them in charge of icebreakers.

The roles and responsibilities can be as unique as the people in your group.
Find a way for them to own it.
Give them a role so that when they miss group, they miss being there.
And when they miss group, something feels missing, and they are missed.

Because you don't just *go* to group. You *are* a group.

But it's not just moving the group to be a group.
It's also about moving the group to be on mission.
This is when we move from *learning about* the Bible to *living out* the Bible.

A church that stays within its four walls is no church at all.
The same can be said of our groups.
If we just sit in the same circle in the same space and never take our group outside of those four walls, we will miss out on a dimension of community and a dynamic of transformation that can only be found when we are serving together.

We have to literally move them out of the living room. Or coffeehouse. Or conference room. Or whatever place you meet.
Move them outside the four walls.
Engage their faith with things outside your circle.

When we come together as a small group, we benefit from face-to-face community. It's the connection that happens when we can look each other in the eye and encourage one another, pray for one another, support one another, and be with one another.

But there is another dimension of community that we find when we are shoulder to shoulder.
Serving together.
On mission together.
Making a difference together.

It's like the small group we find in Mark 2. Four friends who had another friend who was paralyzed on a mat. The four friends refused to simply go to a house to learn what Jesus had to say. They were determined to make a difference in their friend's life.

So they went to pick him up.
Carried him on his mat through the streets of the city.
And when they got to the house where Jesus was teaching, it was standing room only.
The door was completely blocked.
So they took the next obvious route. No, not a window. The roof.
They dug a whole through the roof.
They devised a pulley system of some sort, maybe out of their robes and lowered their paralyzed friend on his mat to the feet of Jesus.

First, Jesus said, "Son, your sins are forgiven."
And because that seemed to ruffle the feathers of some religious people, He followed it up with an even bigger shocking statement: Get up, take up your mat, and walk.

But there is one little detail that is significant.
The Scripture says that Jesus saw "their faith"—the faith of the four friends—and that's what prompted His actions.
Not the faith of the religious people.
Not the faith of the paralyzed man himself.
The faith of the four friends who were willing to go on mission together.

The life of the paralyzed man wasn't changed because he had a face-to-face experience with his four friends.
His life was changed because his four friends decided to get

shoulder to shoulder and sweat a little.

They partnered together to shoulder the burden.
And that partnership changed their friend's life.
Their partnership set the stage for Jesus to show up and show off in a powerful way.

The man walked out with new legs and a new identity because of his friends.
Whose life is being changed because of your group?

The people in that room may not have remembered a word that Jesus said.
But I bet they would always remember the man who got up, slung his mat over his shoulder, and walked out the door.
They didn't just hear the good news Jesus came to bring. They saw it.
How is your group proclaiming the good news of Jesus in practical ways to the world around you?

Jesus told his disciples: "A new command I give you: Love one another. As I have loved you, so you must love one another. By this everyone will know that you are my disciples, if you love one another."

What if our love for one another was so compelling and so profound that it drew others toward Jesus?

When we get outside of our four walls
When we get shoulder to shoulder to bear the burdens of others
When we serve with one another . . .
it changes us,
and it changes the world around us.

Our face-to-face connection is deepened when we link arms shoulder to shoulder.

Move your group outside the four walls.

Journal ✐

Write down the name of every person in your group.
Next to each name, identify one unique gift and one unique
passion that person has.

Make a list of some of the needs you see in your group and in
your larger community/neighborhood.

Match people with potential roles and responsibilities.

3 Move Them to What's Next

As a small group leader, you will find yourself walking with your group through various transitions.

Part of your job as a leader is to look for, anticipate, and serve as a guide through those times.

Remember, you are a tour guide, not a travel agent. So lace up those boots and get ready to go on a journey.

The first category of next steps is the **faith transition**. Your group will likely be an incubator in which the Holy Spirit grows people, matures people, and prepares them for something else.

What's that next step?

Depending on your church tradition, does someone in your group need to take a step of making a decision to follow Jesus, to be baptized, or to be confirmed?
Is someone in your group going to take communion for the first time?
Is someone in your group ready to become a member of a church?

In the area of faith transitions, your role as a small group leader is to guide and celebrate.

Guide means that we talk about spiritual milestones.
We make sure our members know how to take those steps.
Then we walk alongside them and pray for them as they make those decisions.

Celebrate means we applaud and affirm. We are present.
Maybe we even give presents. Or write them a note of encouragement.
We cheer them on. Maybe we even throw a party.

In Luke 15, Jesus said that a party erupts in heaven when one sinner repents. Sounds like a good idea. Maybe that idea is worth replicating in your group, as well.

As leaders, we must guide and celebrate our few in their faith transitions.

The second area of transition is **growth opportunities**.

This could mean going on a mission trip.
Being generous in giving.
Serving on a ministry team.
Making a difference in your neighborhood.
Working with kids or with youth.

As we help our few navigate growth opportunities, our role is to identify and support.

Identify means making sure your few know about opportunities to serve, give, and go.
It means helping your few identify their unique God-given wiring and design.
It means matching their passions with the needs around them.

And then you support. You affirm their growth. You applaud how they are making a difference.

Finally, we also find ourselves helping our few navigate **new life seasons**.

A new job or a lay off.
A new baby coming home or a teenager going to college.
A new marriage or the end of a marriage.
Moving to a new house or perhaps even to a new city.
A sickness or death.
A promotion or a demotion.
A set back. A step back. A comeback.

As small group leaders, our role is to show up and shoulder the burden.

Simply showing up is the best thing you can do.
Being present. Being with. Being there.
People often won't remember what you've said, but they will remember you were there.
You don't need to say the perfect thing; you just need proximity.

Shouldering the burden means we help them keep their faith central to the transition.
We help them take the curves. Think about it, when you come to a curve in the road, you don't speed up. You slow down, pay a little more attention, and drive intentionally and deliberately.

We help them handle the mess.
Whether the transition is a positive step or seems like a setback, those going through the transition need a support network.

Move your few through their life transitions.
Guide them.
Celebrate them.
Support them.
Show up for them.
Shoulder the burden with them.

Move them through life.

One final word about moving.

Every group eventually comes to an end.
You may have a specific time frame for your few and know you will only stay together for a few months or a year.

Other groups seem like they could go on forever. And you may wish that they would.

But people move. People change. People need new relationships in different seasons.

Be intentional with the season you have and be gracious when it's time to transition.

And when it is time to transition, make sure to celebrate the good times, acknowledge the memories, honor one another, and thank God for the work He did in you and through you.

The few you have now will probably not be your few forever.

But they are your few for now. So be present for them. Be with them. Be for them.

But keep an open hand.

When you move them out, you engage them in a bigger story.
You stretch them to a greater capacity.
You challenge them to make a bigger impact.

**Move them to
someone else**

**Move them to be
the church**

**Move them to
what's next**

WHEN YOU
MOVE THEM OUT,
YOU ENGAGE
AUTHENTIC
FAITH.

a few more thoughts

Erastus.

Rufus.

Gaius.

Phoebe.

Priscilla.

Olympas.

Aquilla.

These names probably don't mean anything to us, but they meant the world to Paul. When Paul wrote his letter to the church in Rome, it was his most theological and philosophical book. It would become the most systematic, categorical, and comprehensive declaration of faith in the entire New Testament.

When we turn the page to the last chapter, we find a list of almost three dozen names. After he put the period on his statement of faith, he let the credits roll. He listed the people who had shaped him and formed him, the people who had invested in him, the people who had taken a risk on him, and the people who had been crazy enough to join him.

The names we find in Romans 16 are those who had served as Paul's mentors, disciples, teammates, and spiritual family. He acknowledged that his life had depended upon the generosity, prayers, and encouragement of these people and that even his theology could not be formed in a vacuum. Paul could not make his declaration of faith or tell his spiritual journey without including the names of these people.

All of us have a Romans 16 list. Mine includes the names of Sunday school teachers, educators, pastors, coaches, my parents' friends, and my friends' parents. Because of the way they invested in me, believed in me, encouraged me, prayed for me, and taught me, I can't tell my story of faith without including their names. Who will be on your list? Who are the people that have shaped your understanding of faith? Who has walked life's journey with you and pointed out the fingerprints of God along the way? A coach, a youth pastor, a friend, a grandparent?

But it's not simply about the names on our list. We also need to ask ourselves whose Romans 16 list will include our names? Who have you walked with, prayed for, and encouraged? Who have you pointed toward Jesus, reminding them of who God is and who they are in light of his character? Who can't tell their story without including your name?

Have we prioritized people such that we are building Romans 16 lists for ourselves and for future generations?

Will our group members have a vibrant faith and a story to tell? Help them build their list.

When you lead small you . . .
Connect authentic faith
Clarify authentic faith
Inspire authentic faith
Engage authentic faith

That's a really big job. It's not the kind of job you sign up for if you're just looking to kill an extra hour a week doing something mindless—there are a lot of other great options for that.

This is a journey you sign up for because
You want to do something significant.
You are ready to make a difference.
You care about nurturing authentic faith in a few people.
You want to play a role in the next chapter God is writing in those around you.

And as a small group leader, you will make a difference.

How can we be so confident?

Your job as a small group leader can all be boiled down to one very simple thought. One phrase. One idea.

In fact, bookmark this page.

So, when you feel overwhelmed, when you feel stuck, when you feel paralyzed, open the book to this page and know that all you have to remember is

Your few are not problems to be solved.
They are people to be loved.

When you love them, you will *connect* by showing up predictably, mentally and randomly.
When you love them, you will naturally create a safe place for them to *clarify their faith.*
When you love them, you will want to *inspire* them through your example.
When you love them, you will *engage* their faith with things outside of your circle.

The best way to love your few is to lead them toward big change in small ways.

LIVE A
BETTER
STORY